P9-DMQ-960

RIDGEFIELD LIBRARY
472 MAIN STREET
RIDGEFIELD, CONN. 06877

APR 1 9 2010

Fact Finders®

Explore the Biomes

EXPLORE THE

Desert

by Kay Jackson

Consultant:
Dr. Sandra Mather
Professor Emerita of Geology and Astronomy
West Chester University
West Chester, Pennsylvania

Capstone
press®

Mankato, Minnesota

Fact Finders is published by Capstone Press,
151 Good Counsel Drive, P.O. Box 669, Mankato, Minnesota 56002.
www.capstonepress.com

Copyright © 2007 by Capstone Press. All rights reserved.
No part of this publication may be reproduced in whole or in part, or stored in a retrieval system,
or transmitted in any form or by any means, electronic, mechanical, photocopying, recording, or
otherwise, without written permission of the publisher.
For information regarding permission, write to Capstone Press,
151 Good Counsel Drive, P.O. Box 669, Dept. R, Mankato, Minnesota 56002.
Printed in the United States of America

Library of Congress Cataloging-in-Publication Data
Jackson, Kay, 1959–
    Explore the desert / by Kay Jackson.
        p. cm.—(Fact finders. Explore the biomes)
    Includes bibliographical references and index.
    ISBN-13: 978-0-7368-6404-6 (hardcover)
    ISBN-10: 0-7368-6404-0 (hardcover)
    ISBN-13: 978-0-7368-9627-6 (softcover pbk.)
    ISBN-10: 0-7368-9627-9 (softcover pbk.)
    1. Desert ecology—Juvenile literature. I. Title. II. Series.
QH541.5.D4J33 2007
577.54—dc22   2006004109

Summary: Discusses the plants, animals, and characteristics of the desert biome.

Editorial Credits
Erika L. Shores, editor; Juliette Peters, designer; Tami Collins, map illustrator;
    Wanda Winch, photo researcher

Photo Credits
Bruce Coleman Inc./Bob & Clara Calhoun, 17 (kangaroo rat); Jeff Foott, 18
Comstock Images, cover (background)
Corbis/Douglas Peebles, 24; Julia Waterlow/Eye Ubiquitous, 11; Kevin Schafer, 12;
    Martin Harvey, 21; Paul Hardy, 5
Courtesy of Kay Jackson, 32
©The Field Museum/neg. #GN90737_3c, 29, Robert Zingg, 29 (inset)
Houserstock/Dave G. Houser, 9
James P. Rowan, 15, 18 (scorpion), 27 (cactus)
Minden Pictures/Michael & Patricia Fogden, 16
Peter Arnold/Fred Bruemmer, 6
Photodisc, cover (foreground); Siede Preis, 1, 3, 20, 25 (bottom), 30
Photo Researchers Inc./David Hosking, 13
Shutterstock, 26; Dave Stubblefield, 10 (yucca); Doxa, 26; Gianluca Figliola Fantini, 12–13
    (cactus fruits); Hashim Pudiyapura, 4; Jason Cheever, 9 (bottom); Jim Parkin, 6–7; Magdalena
    Bujak, 27 (iguana); Michael Fuery, 8; Nelson Sirlin, 10–11, 22–23; Rodney Mehring, 13 (mesquite
    tree seed pods), 22 (grasshopper)
SuperStock/age fotostock, 25
Tom Stack & Associates Inc./Joe McDonald, 17
Visuals Unlimited/Rick and Nora Bowers, 19

Table of Contents

CHAPTER 1

A Dry Land

A camel slowly walks across the hot, dry sand. Sunshine blazes down on the camel's rider. Wind blows the sand around them into giant dunes. The rider sips water. But the camel will travel many miles before it needs to take a drink. Its body is made to live in a land where water is hard to find.

Animals like the camel are suited to live in the harsh conditions of a desert. The world's deserts are the driest places on earth. Deserts get less than 10 inches (25 centimeters) of rain each year. Desert air is so dry, raindrops often **evaporate** before they reach the ground.

camels

Camels use fat stored in humps on their backs when they need to go without food and water.

The Atacama Desert in South America is the driest place on earth. Rain might fall only once every 20 years.

The Desert Biome

In the desert **biome**, a community of unique plants and animals have adapted to the dry **climate**. Desert plants and animals depend on each other for survival. Desert plants provide shelter and food for desert animals. Animals help plants by spreading their seeds throughout the desert. But some deserts have such harsh conditions that almost no plants and animals live there.

Field Note

Where are deserts?

- Africa
- Antarctica
- Arctic areas
- Asia
- Australia
- North America
- South America

N
W — E
S

☐ desert

Deserts can be cold or hot. Antarctica is a cold desert. Temperatures stay far below freezing in winter. Thick fur or feathers protect animals from the cold.

In hot deserts, animals hide under rocks or in holes during the day. Plants have adapted to hot deserts too. The leaves of some desert trees curl up during the hottest parts of the day. They save water this way.

burrowing owls

CHAPTER 2

Desert Plants

Splash! Raindrops splatter on the desert. Desert plants have waited months, maybe even years, for the rain. Rain brings life to the desert. After a few days, hidden seeds start to sprout. Soon, spiky spinifex grasses pop up from the ground. Cactuses soak up as much water as they can.

In just a month, wildflowers cover desert hillsides. Bright blossoms sprout from thorny cactuses. Bees zip between flowers. Antelope nibble on new green leaves.

spinifex grasses

Bright yellow flowers burst open on a prickly pear cactus.

ocotillo

Saving Water

Because rain is rare in the desert, plants must store water. Prickly cactuses have ways to live in the desert. Shallow roots spread out to collect water across a wide area of the ground. Hard, waxy skin holds in water. Sharp spines keep thirsty animals away.

FACT!
The yucca plant is food for many desert dwellers. Jackrabbits nibble their leaves. Gophers eat their roots. Birds and mice snatch up yucca seeds.

Saguaros and other cactuses are a type of succulent plant. Succulents store water.

The nara plant grows in the dry Namib Desert. The bush's roots store water.

In Africa's Namib Desert, small, leafless bushes dot the brown, rocky ground. The twisted gray branches make the plants look dead. But they aren't. To live in this harsh land, the nara plant has thick roots deep underground that store water.

Finding Water

Water in the desert doesn't last long. Blistering heat and sunshine quickly evaporate the water. Tree leaves shrivel and die once the water is gone. But the dead leaves on the Joshua tree don't fall off. The leaves shade the trunk and keep it from dying in the hot sun.

A Joshua tree grows tall in the Mojave Desert in the western United States.

cactus fruit

A desert mouse scurries across the hot sand searching for seeds to eat.

mesquite tree
seed pods

Desert life changes during the dry season. Seed pods and fruits take the place of bright flowers. Desert animals eat plants to give them enough water to survive until the next rainfall. Tortoises munch on juicy cactus fruits.

The dry seed pods of a mesquite tree rustle in the wind and drop on the ground. A field mouse snatches up a pod. Seeds in the pod have water locked inside their smooth shells.

CHAPTER 3

Desert Animals

Mice and tortoises are just a couple of the animals that have learned to survive in the desert. Desert bugs are fierce fighters. They have to be tough to live in the dry land. Scorpions jab their **prey** with poisonous stingers. The stinkbug shoots enemies with a smelly spray.

The desert tarantula has stinging hairs on its **abdomen**. If a bird or snake gets too close, the tarantula flicks hairs into the animal's eyes and blinds it.

Other desert insects are gentler. Butterflies flit between flowers. They drink the blossoms' nectar. Colorful butterflies stand out in the brown desert.

A tarantula hunts small insects in the hot desert.

15

Scaly, spiky, and bumpy **reptiles** thrive in the desert. They have watertight skin. Their skin doesn't sweat, so they don't lose water.

Scritch, scritch. The claws of a lizard scrape against the sand. The nervous lizard scrambles toward a bush. A nearby snake slithers to a stop. The snake senses the lizard. With a snap of its powerful jaws, the snake grabs the lizard and swallows it whole.

A sidewinding adder snake swallows a lizard in Africa's Namib Desert.

When a Gila monster bites its prey, deadly venom from its jaws flows into the animal.

kangaroo rat

Another hunter crawls along the desert floor. A Gila monster searches for a meal. The red and black lizard finds a kangaroo rat hiding beneath a bush. With quick gulps, the Gila monster gobbles up its prey.

Coyotes hunt at night in the desert when it is cooler.

Desert Animals Hunt at Night

During the hot day, many animals hide in cool burrows or under shady rocks. But when the sun goes down, desert animals come out.

High above in the dark sky, a brown bat flies overhead. In the shadows, a lean coyote sniffs the air. It catches the scent of a mouse.

Field Note

Scorpions are night hunters.

- Size: 2 to 3 inches (5 to 8 centimeters) long
- Color: yellow-brown
- Food: insects, spiders, other scorpions

18

From a small hole in a giant saguaro cactus, an elf owl's round eyes scan the ground below. A speckled grasshopper leaps from a bush. In a swift dive, the tiny owl snatches the grasshopper and silently flaps back to its nest.

As the sun rises, night animals go back to their nests and burrows. During the night, few animals found water, but they aren't thirsty. To live in the dry land, desert animals need very little water.

An elf owl peeks out from its nest in a saguaro cactus.

CHAPTER 4

People and the Desert

A man wearing a blue turban guides his camel across the sandy floor of Africa's Sahara Desert. The man belongs to a group of people called the Tuareg, the Blue People of the desert. The dark dye of their turbans rubs off onto their skin.

For thousands of years, the Tuaregs were nomads, moving from place to place. The Tuaregs were also traders. Their **caravans** of camels took goods, like spices and grains, across the Sahara Desert.

In recent times, many Tuaregs have settled along the edges of the Sahara. Droughts made it hard to find food for their camels. Wars made it dangerous to live in some places of the desert.

wheat grains

Tuaregs use camels to carry goods long distances across the desert.

desert grasshopper

People Affect the Desert

People in the desert must be careful to protect the plants and animals living there. People might not realize the effect they have on the desert. By destroying desert plants, people harm desert animals. Animals that eat the plants no longer have food or shelter. If people kill desert animals, like tarantulas or other spiders, larger animals that eat the spiders have to find other food to eat.

People who hike in deserts should stay on trails so they don't disrupt plants and animals.

Even though a rocky, dry desert looks tough, it's a delicate place. Hikers should stay on trails in the desert. When people wander off trails, they might accidentally crush a cactus. Hikers who aren't careful might trample over the burrows of mice or lizards causing the animals' underground homes to collapse.

FACT!

Aliens have come to deserts in the United States. Alien plants, that is. The tumbleweed and salt cedar are not native to American deserts. Both plants were accidentally brought from Asia and Europe in the 1800s and early 1900s.

Protecting the Desert

Some people don't come to deserts just to hike. They want to live there. In the United States, desert cities are growing fast. Each year thousands of people move to desert states like Arizona and Nevada. Malls, roads, houses, and stores are built and crowd out desert animals and plants.

Las Vegas, Nevada, sprawls across thousands of acres of desert land.

Death Valley
National Park

Homeland of the Timbisha Shoshone

NATIONAL
PARK
SERVICE

The U.S. government protects desert areas by setting up national parks.

To make sure deserts don't disappear, countries and states make laws to set aside land. In these protected areas, people aren't allowed to build roads or homes. It's against the law to harm any of the plants or animals that live there.

CHAPTER 5

Desert Field Guide

Where to find deserts:

Africa, Antarctica, Arctic areas, Asia, Australia, North America, South America

CLIMATE:

- temperature range: in hot deserts, 85 to 100 degrees Fahrenheit (29 to 38 degrees Celsius)
- annual precipitation: less than 10 inches (25 centimeters)

BUGS:

ants, bees, black widow spiders, butterflies, scorpions, tarantulas, termites

Question:

Where do some animals go during the hottest part of the day in a desert?

- **Common mammals:** bats, coyotes, fennec foxes, gophers, jackals, kangaroo rats, mice, wolves
- **Common reptiles:** Gila monsters, iguanas, lizards, rattlesnakes, tortoises
- **Common birds:** cactus wrens, Gila woodpeckers, hawks, owls, roadrunners

PLANTS:

birdcage plants, brittlebush shrubs, cactuses, creosote bushes, Joshua trees, mesquite shrubs and trees, nara plants, spinifex grasses, yuccas

Desert products:
oil found underground, fruit from some types of cactuses, baskets, mats, ropes

CHAPTER 6

A Scientist at Work

At the southern tip of the island of Madagascar lies one of the world's strangest deserts. The Spiny Desert is a place of twisted trees and bushes, all covered in sharp thorns.

Dr. Steve Goodman, a biologist with Chicago's Field Museum of Natural History, has studied the plants and animals of Madagascar's Spiny Desert for the last 14 years. When Goodman wanted to find out more about Madagascar's mouse lemurs, he went camping.

Goodman spent time in the desert studying the lemurs up close. Goodman recorded what he saw, heard, smelled, and touched. He shared what he learned about the tiny animals with the government of Madagascar. His research taught people how to protect the mouse lemur by making sure the desert plants it eats are not destroyed.

GLOSSARY

abdomen (AB-duh-muhn)—the end section of an insect's body

biome (BUY-ome)—an area with a particular type of climate, and certain plants and animals that live there

caravan (KA-ruh-van)—a group of people traveling together

climate (KLYE-mit)—the usual weather in a place

evaporate (e-VAP-uh-rate)—the action of a liquid changing into vapor or a gas; heat causes water to evaporate.

prey (PRAY)—an animal hunted by another animal

reptile (REP-tile)—a cold-blooded animal with a backbone; scales cover a reptile's body.

INTERNET SITES

FactHound offers a safe, fun way to find Internet sites related to this book. All of the sites on FactHound have been researched by our staff.

Here's how:

1. Visit *www.facthound.com*

2. Choose your grade level.

3. Type in this book ID **0736864040** for age-appropriate sites. You may also browse subjects by clicking on letters, or by clicking on pictures and words.

4. Click on the **Fetch It** button.

FactHound will fetch the best sites for you!

READ MORE

Ganeri, Anita. *Deserts.* Science Files. Earth. Milwaukee: Gareth Stevens, 2003.

Kallen, Stuart A. *Life in a Desert*. Ecosystems. San Diego: Kidhaven Press, 2004.

Lawerence, Katherine. *Life in the Desert*. Life in Extreme Environments. New York: Rosen Central, 2004.

INDEX

ABOUT THE AUTHOR

Kay Jackson

Kay Jackson writes nonfiction books for children. Kay lived and taught for seven years near Phoenix, Arizona, in the middle of the Sonoran Desert. With her sixth grade students and family, she has hiked and explored that amazing desert from Tucson to Flagstaff. Now, Kay lives and writes in Tulsa, Oklahoma, close to the last bit of North America's tallgrass prairie.